MARGARET MORGAN
and
MARY MORGAN PEDLOW

Memorial

RIVERSIDE PUBLIC LIBRARY

Transportation & Communication Series

Highways and Freeways

Arlene Bourgeois Molzahn

Enslow Publishers, Inc.

40 Industrial Road
Box 398
Berkeley Heights, NJ 07922
USA

PO Box 38
Aldershot
Hants GU12 6BP
UK

http://www.enslow.com

To my beloved father, Joseph Anthony, who traveled on Wisconsin's highways for thirty-five years.

Copyright © 2002 by Enslow Publishers, Inc.

Library of Congress Cataloging-in-Publication Data

Molzahn, Arlene Bourgeois.
    Highways and freeways / Arlene Bourgeois Molzahn.
        p. cm. — (Transportation & communication series)
    Includes bibliographical references and index.
    ISBN 0-7660-1891-1
    Summary: Examines the history of roads, the purpose of different types
of roadways, the people who work on them, and ways to make better roads
in the future.
    1. Roads—Juvenile literature. [1. Roads.] I. Title. II. Series.
TE149 .M65 2002
625.7—dc21   2001004204

Printed in the United States of America

10 9 8 7 6 5 4 3 2 1

Illustration credits: Alaska State Library, p. 6 (top); Corel Corporation, pp. 1, 2, 4, 7, 9 (top), 10, 12 (bottom), 13, 14, 15, 16, 17, 18, 19 (top), 20, 21, 22, 23, 24, 27, 28, 29, 30, 31, 32, 34, 35, 36, 37, 38, 40, 41; Dover Publications, Inc., p. 26 (top); Hemera Technologies, Inc. 1997-2000, pp. 5, 6 (bottom), 9 (bottom), 11, 12 (top), 14 (top), 20 (top), 25, 26 (bottom), 28 (bottom), 29 (top), 33, 36 (top) 39; Library of Congress, p.8, 19 (bottom).

Cover Illustration: © Corbis Corp. Digital Stock

Contents

Chapter 1

The Alaska Highway

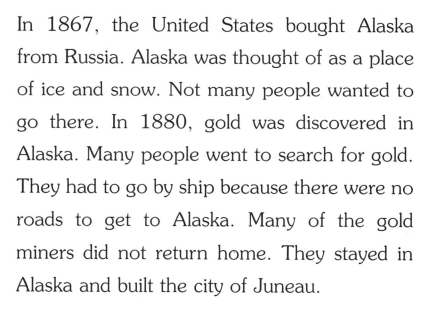

In 1867, the United States bought Alaska from Russia. Alaska was thought of as a place of ice and snow. Not many people wanted to go there. In 1880, gold was discovered in Alaska. Many people went to search for gold. They had to go by ship because there were no roads to get to Alaska. Many of the gold miners did not return home. They stayed in Alaska and built the city of Juneau.

In 1896, gold was discovered in Klondike Valley in the Yukon Territory of Canada. Again, people traveled by ship to Alaska. Then they went over land through Alaska to

The United States bought Alaska from Russia in 1867.

Gold was discovered in Alaska in the late 1800s. These men are searching for gold.

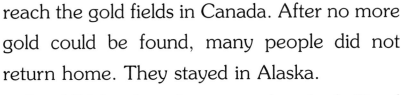

reach the gold fields in Canada. After no more gold could be found, many people did not return home. They stayed in Alaska.

In 1941, the Japanese bombed Pearl Harbor, Hawaii. That was the start of the war between the United States and Japan. In 1942, Japanese bombers attacked the American naval base in the Aleutian Islands of Alaska. Japanese troops captured two islands, Attu and Kiska.

The United States needed a highway between Alaska and the other forty-eight states. This highway would be a military supply route that would help protect Alaska. It would have to go through the country of Canada. The government of Canada gave the United States the right to build the highway.

The United States Army Corps of Engineers was given the job to build the highway. Road building equipment was moved to the city of Dawson Creek, British Columbia, Canada. Most people thought it would take years to build the highway. But the Army engineers finished the highway in just eight months. It went from Dawson Creek, British Columbia, to Delta Junction, Alaska. Then the Richardson Highway

The U.S. Army Corps of Engineers started building the Alaska Highway in British Columbia, Canada, seen here.

connected Delta Junction to Fairbanks, Alaska. The road cost about $140,000,000.

In 1943, with the help of the Navy, United States soldiers recaptured the islands of Attu and Kiska. Soldiers and supplies could now be sent to Alaska using the new highway. The recapture of those islands was called The One Thousand Mile War.

At first, the highway was known as the Alcan Highway. But soon people began calling it the Alaska Highway. There were 1,221 miles of the highway that crossed the country of Canada. Canadians were given that part of the highway in 1946. The highway has been straightened so that now the length of the highway in Canada is 1,196 miles.

The Alaska Highway was once called the Alcan Highway. This photo was taken in 1942.

Today the total length of the highway is 1,397 miles.

Most of the highway surface is made of either concrete or asphalt. Other parts have a surface of packed gravel. The highway has some rough sections, but these are clearly marked for travelers.

People can travel freely across Canada on the Alaska Highway. But, it is very cold in the winter. Snowstorms can make traveling dangerous. In spring, the thawing of the roadway makes travel hard.

This is a part of the Alaska Highway.

Early May to late September is the best time to travel on the highway. The scenery is beautiful. Snow-capped mountains, lakes, and many trees can be seen from the highway. Travelers are also treated to meadows of wild flowers along the way.

Many Types of Roads

Today there are many different types of roads. Local roads are the roads that are found in front of your home. They connect your house to the rest of the community. Often these roads do not have a lot of traffic. If you live in a city, your local road is called a street. Most city streets have two driving lanes in the center. They sometimes have a lane for parking on each side of the street.

Roads that connect small communities to each other are called secondary roads.

Primary highways connect large cities. Many cars, trucks, and buses travel on them.

Local roads are the roads found in front of your home, like this one on the left.

Most primary highways have four or more traffic lanes.

Freeways or superhighways are another kind of highway. Vehicles can go on or go off a freeway only at certain places called interchanges. Ramps are built at interchanges for vehicles to get off or on the highway. Interchanges have overpasses and underpasses. These are built over and under the highway. Overpasses are

This is a rustic road.

also built over railroad tracks so that traffic does not have to stop for trains.

All freeways are not really free. On some freeways, travelers are charged money, called a toll, for use of the highway. These freeways are called toll roads. The toll money is used to help pay for the freeways.

Roads can have many different kinds of surfaces. Roads that have very little traffic have gravel surfaces. These roads wind through areas where very few people live. Sometimes these roads are called rustic roads.

Heavily traveled roads need hard surfaces. Chemicals and tar are mixed with small stones to make asphalt. Road builders use asphalt to surface many roads. Trucks bring hot asphalt to a paving machine. The paving machine spreads the hot mix on the roadbed. Large

Some roads go through mountains.

This crew is getting ready to spread asphalt onto a new road.

rollers smooth the asphalt. The asphalt cools quickly. In a few hours, people can drive on the road. These asphalt-paved roads are sometimes called blacktop roads.

Major highways, such as freeways and primary highways, have surfaces of concrete.

Concrete is a mixture of cement, sand, water, and gravel. Concrete is best used for busy highways. It lasts the longest of any road

surface. Concrete highways have fewer potholes and need fewer repairs than asphalt roads. Concrete surfaces reflect light, making it easier for drivers to see when driving at night. Concrete is also the most expensive material for paving road surfaces.

Road builders like to build roads that are straight and level. Sometimes tunnels have to be built. Some tunnels go through mountains and some go under rivers. Sometimes tunnels go under busy streets.

Roads do not stop at rivers. There are many types of bridges that let people cross rivers, railroad tracks, and other roads. All of them let people have the freedom to travel.

There are many types of bridges that let people cross water, railroad tracks, and other roads.

Chapter 3

From Trails to Superhighways

Wild animals traveled from feeding grounds to watering holes. They used the same paths over and over. Soon they had worn trails through fields and forests. Long ago, people followed these trails to hunt for food and to find water. Early explorers also used animal paths and trails as they traveled through new lands.

After the wheel was invented, people began to travel farther. They began trading goods from town to town. Soon people began to make their own roads. These roads were

Animals use paths as roads to find water and food.

17

Before roads, people would travel on narrow dirt paths.

straighter and usually wider than the animal paths.

Early rulers built roads for their soldiers and tax collectors. They needed to be able to reach all their land. Roads made it easier for the soldiers to protect the country from its enemies. Roads were needed to help soldiers keep peace among the people.

Many rulers built short roads in areas of their countries. But rulers of China were the first to build roads throughout their country. By the year 230, nearly 20,000 miles of roads existed in the Chinese Empire.

The Romans were excellent builders of early roads. Their road building began about 2,500 years ago. Their roads were built on a solid base. The stone blocks they used were placed a little higher in the center of the road. When it rained, the water could run off easily. They also built ditches on the sides of their roads to carry the water away. The Romans built over 50,000 miles of roads in their empire. Many of their roads are still being used today.

Corduroy roads were built in

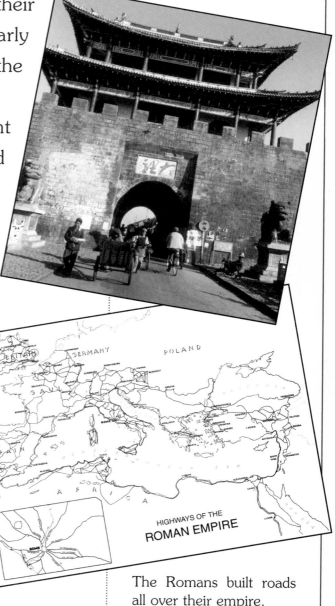

The Chinese were the first to build roads throughout their country.

HIGHWAYS OF THE
ROMAN EMPIRE

The Romans built roads all over their empire.

The automobile helped bring changes to how roads were made.

places where there were many trees. These roads were made by placing logs crosswise over the roadway. Corduroy roads were very bumpy. They were also very slippery when wet. There were many corduroy roads during the colonial days in America.

The automobile brought about changes in the roads. Earth, stone, or log roads were poor roads for cars. In 1908, the first concrete highway in the United States was laid in

Detroit, Michigan. The need for paved roads grew as more people began buying automobiles. By 1924, the United States had over 31,000 miles of concrete highways. The United States continued to build highways. Soon people could travel almost anywhere.

As more people began to use the roads, rules had to be made. In the United States and Canada, cars must drive on the right side of the road. In Great Britain, Japan, and Australia, cars must drive on the left side of the road.

Red, yellow, and green are the colors used for electric traffic lights. Red means stop, yellow means wait or get ready to stop, and green means go. The first traffic lights in the United States were put up in New York City in 1918. The first patent for a traffic light was given to Garrett A. Morgan in 1923. This

In some countries, people drive on the left side of the road.

traffic light had three positions. They were stop, go, and a position that made all the cars stop so people could walk. Soon traffic lights directed the movement of cars and trucks in all large cities in the United States.

Less traveled roads have traffic signs. These signs tell drivers when to stop. The signs also tell drivers how fast they can go on the road. Some roads even have signs that tell drivers to watch out for animals, like deer.

The first traffic lights in the United States were put up in New York City in 1918.

In many places, drivers have to watch for animals that might cross the highway.

Chapter 4

Improving the Highways

Many people helped our roads and highways become what they are today. One was Pierre Tresaguet, a French road engineer. In 1760, he came up with the idea of putting down three layers of different size stones. This helped to form a harder surface for the roads.

Thomas Telford was a Scottish engineer. In the early 1800s, he put a fine layer of small stones over his roads. Then he had heavy wheels roll over the surface to pack down the stones. This filled in the gaps and made the surface waterproof.

In 1845, John McAdam was the first to

Many people helped plan and build this highway.

Henry Ford, above, found a way to make cars, like this one below, faster and cheaper.

seal the road surfaces with tar. This made the roads smooth and dust free. It also made the roads last longer.

In 1862, Colonel Pierpoint, an Englishman, built an island in the center of a street in Liverpool, England. Islands are still being built in the center of streets today. These islands help people to cross busy streets. Islands also separate cars going in opposite directions.

Henry Ford found a new way to make cars faster and cheaper. Many people started driving cars. Narrow dusty roads were not good enough for cars. New and wider roads with hard surfaces had to be built. More roads were needed because people wanted to travel to far away places.

Soon many highways had been built. People did not always know which highway to take. In 1917, A. R. Hirst, from the Wisconsin Highway Department, suggested that all highways be numbered. In 1925, the United States began numbering the highways.

Interstate highways go from state to state. Highways going east to west have even numbers. Highways going north to south have odd numbers. New maps were made showing the highways with their numbers. This made it much easier for people who did a lot of traveling. Today all roads are named or numbered. Travelers can find the right road to take by looking at a map.

Signs along highways are important for travelers. They tell travelers how far it is to the next city. Speed signs show how fast a vehicle can travel on the highway. Billboards are big advertising signs that tell about things a traveler can find in the next city.

Years ago, asphalt for roads cost a lot of money. Today scientists have found a way to recycle the asphalt surface from old roadbeds. A machine

Highways have signs like this to tell travelers what road they are on or how fast they are allowed to drive.

This billboard lets people know they are in Nebraska.

removes the asphalt from the road and grinds it up. Fresh asphalt is then mixed with the old ground up asphalt. A paving machine then puts the asphalt mixture back on the road surface. Next, huge power rollers pack down the asphalt. This makes the old road like new. Soon it is smooth and ready for vehicles to travel on.

In 1956, Congress passed the Federal-Aid Highway Act. This gave money from the United States government to states for highway building. States began building many new highways. Old highways were made better. Traveling throughout the United States became much easier.

A highway that is built in a scenic area may have a turn off called a scenic overlook. A scenic overlook lets travelers stop and look at the beautiful scenery without slowing the flow of traffic.

Busy highways have rest stops. Rest areas

Signs like this one show travelers that scenic places are nearby.

have rest rooms, water, and sometimes picnic tables for travelers to use. Usually there is an information board with a map of the area. Sometimes information and pictures about interesting things in the area are also posted.

In hilly or mountainous areas, highways have runaway truck ramps. These ramps are very steep and have sandy surfaces. Big trucks sometimes need help slowing down or stopping. The driver can drive onto the ramp and safely stop the truck.

Today, civil engineers have set standards for roads. They want to make sure that roads are safe. They oversee highway projects as the roadways are being built.

Some highways have beautiful scenery and interesting wildlife around them (left).

Rest areas give travelers a chance to picnic, get information, or use rest rooms.

Chapter 5

Many Types of Highway Jobs

Many workers are needed to build a new highway. A lot of work needs to be done before the building of a highway can even begin.

Planners are the first people needed. They set up electric counters to see how much traffic there is on the highway. Crowded highways can be very dangerous. When the counters show that the highway is too busy, a new highway is needed.

Next, planners must prove to lawmakers that tax money is needed for the road. After that, surveyors and engineers begin to work.

Backhoes can dig large amounts of dirt at once (left).

Huge earth movers help clear away dirt.

Road scrapers are also used in making a new highway.

Together they look for the best place to put the highway. Then the land is bought.

Huge machines are put to work to clear the land. They must cut down trees and bushes. Buildings must be moved or torn down. Large trucks are needed to haul all these things away.

Next, come backhoes and bulldozers. These big machines can dig large amounts of dirt at once. They level hills and move big rocks.

Dump trucks bring gravel for the roadbed. The road graders move the gravel in a certain way. The roadbed must be smooth and a little higher in the center. Then rain will run off the highway quickly. Heavy rollers are used to pack the gravel down.

Next, a movable concrete plant is set up at a halfway point along the highway to be paved. Large dump trucks are filled with wet concrete. The concrete is hauled to the paving machine. Steel rods are placed along the edge of the roadway. The concrete is dumped in front of the paving machine as it slowly moves along. The machine spreads the concrete evenly on the highway. As it moves, it places the steel rods where the joints in the highway will be made. The steel rods make the highway stronger. The new highway is sprayed with a chemical to help the concrete harden.

Road graders move the gravel a certain way to smooth the roadbed.

Grass is then planted on the sides of the highway. Sometimes workers need to plant trees and shrubs, too. This helps keep the noise of the traffic from bothering nearby houses.

Heavy rollers are used to pack the gravel down.

Depending on the kind of chemicals that are added to the concrete, it could take from

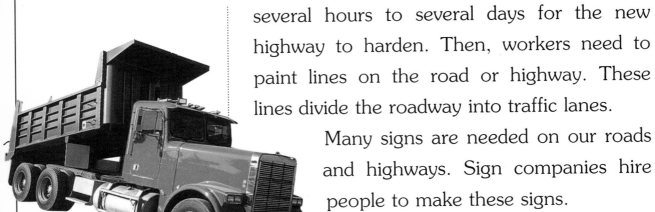

several hours to several days for the new highway to harden. Then, workers need to paint lines on the road or highway. These lines divide the roadway into traffic lanes.

Many signs are needed on our roads and highways. Sign companies hire people to make these signs.

Workers are needed to make the machines that are used in road building. Workers are also needed to drive these machines.

Here an overpass is being built.

Mechanics are needed to keep the machines in good working order. They are also needed when a machine breaks down.

After the highway is finished, police officers are needed to patrol the new highway. This means that cities and states might need to hire more police officers.

Highways and roads need to be kept in good driving condition. Litter has to be picked up. Holes and cracks must be filled. Sometimes highways must be resurfaced. In many places, winter storms bring ice and snow. Snowplows are needed to remove the snow. Salt and sand are spread on the roads and highways to help melt the ice. People must work all year long to keep roads and highways in good driving condition. Building highways and keeping them in good condition provides jobs for thousands of people.

Roads must be kept in good condition.

Chapter 6

Better and Safer Highways

Many people love to travel. Some may feel that traveling by car or motor home is the best way to see the country. City officials want to have superhighways leading to their city. Good highways bring many people who spend a lot of money. This is good for business and it helps their city to grow. People also travel for business. There will always be a need for good highways.

The need for trucking gets larger each year. This means more large semi-trucks will be traveling on our highways. More and better highways are going to be needed.

Highways (left) lead to and from different cities.

More superhighways are planned for the future.

More superhighways are being built. These highways are mostly four or more lanes. They are divided highways. Cars on one section of the highway all go in one direction. On another section of the highway, the cars travel in the opposite direction. Superhighways are made to go as straight as possible. All sharp curves are cut out and steep hills are cut down. Tunnels are made to go through hills and mountains. Also, new and wider bridges are being built.

Future highways may depend on the types of cars that we will be driving. We do have electric powered cars today. Electric cars do not go very fast. They need their batteries recharged very often. Someday the electric car will be made better. These cars may need a different type of highway.

Buses and trains may become a more

popular way to travel. This would cut down the number of cars and trucks on the highways.

Future highways might have more and better lighting. This will help make traveling safer. More and better noise barriers will be built. These barriers will protect the people living near noisy highways.

Scientists are trying to find new ways to remove snow and ice from highways. This is important for people who travel in winter in places where it snows. Scientists hope to find chemicals that will cause less damage to both road surfaces and to vehicles. Some of the chemicals used today cause vehicles to rust.

Highways will always be important in countries where many vehicles are used. Highways let us travel to many different places, whether for business or for fun.

Scientists are looking for new ways to remove snow from highways. Snowplows are one way of removing a lot of snow.

Timeline

450 B.C.—Romans begin building roads throughout their empire.

230 A.D.—Nearly 20,000 miles of roads are built in the country of China.

1760—Several layers of gravel are used to harden the surface of the roads.

1845—Road surfaces are sealed with tar.

1908—One of the first concrete highways is laid.

1916—The United States government helps states pay for highway building.

1918—The first traffic lights are used to direct the flow of traffic in New York City.

1923—Garrett A. Morgan is granted a patent for a traffic signal.

1925—Highways in the United States are numbered to help travelers.

Timeline

1938—Building begins on the first turnpike in the United States.

1950—Great efforts are made to improve highways in the United States.

1956—The Federal-Aid Highway Act is passed to help states pay for road building.

2000—The United States has about 3,900,000 miles of roads.

Words to Know

asphalt—A dark-colored material obtained from oil; when mixed with sand it is used to surface roads.

backhoe—A tractor-like machine, with a bucket at the end of a long arm, that is used for digging.

bulldozer—A tractor with a blade that looks like a large shovel on the front.

concrete—A mixture of cement, sand, water, and gravel.

contractor—A person who agrees to do a job for a certain price.

engineer—A person who studied in special schools and who knows a lot about how to plan and build things.

equipment—Supplies and things that are needed.

Words to Know

mechanic—A worker who keeps machines in good working condition and who fixes machines that have broken down.

recycle—To use something over again.

superhighways—Highways that have four or more lanes going in one direction.

surveyor—A person who measures land and can draw a map of the area.

Learn More About
Highways and Freeways

Books

Adams, Georgie. *Highway Builders*. New York: Annick Press Ltd., 1996.

Armentrout, David and Patricia. *Diggers*. Vero Beach, Fla.: Rourke Book Company, 1995.

Butterfield, Moira. *Bulldozers*. New York: Dorling Kindersley, 1995.

Genat, Robert. *Road Construction*. Osceola, Wisc.: Motorbooks International Pub., 1995.

Hill, Lee Sullivan. *Roads Take Us Home*. Minneapolis, Minn.: Carolrhoda Books, Inc., 1997.

Kalman, Bobbie and Petrina Gentile. *Dirt Movers*. New York: Crabtree Pub. Co., 1994.

Pluckrose, Teri Gower. *Building a Road*. Danbury, Conn.: Franklin Watts, 1999.

Rogers, Hal. *Earthmovers*. Eden Prairie, Minn.: The Child's World, Inc., 2000.

Learn More About
Highways and Freeways

Internet Addresses

Historic California U.S. Highways

<http://gbcnet.com/ushighways/>

Learn about some historic highways.

Build a Model Plank Road

<http://www.sos.state.mi.us/history/museum/
kidstuff/settling/build.html>

*Have fun making your own plank road out of craft sticks
from this Michigan Historical Center Web site.*

Historic Alaska Highway: A Road Building Epic

<http://www.northeasternbc.com/historic.html>

Find out more on the Alaska Highway.

Index